Rainbow

My World

I LIVE HERE!

By Gladys Rosa-Mendoza • Illustrations by Lindy Burnett

WINDMILL
BOOKS ™
New York

Published in 2011 by Windmill Books, LLC
303 Park Avenue South, Suite # 1280, New York, NY 10010-3657

Adaptations to North American Edition © 2011 Windmill Books, LLC
First published by me+mi publishing, inc. © 2001
Text and illustrations copyright © me+mi publishing, inc., 2001

CREDITS:
Author: Gladys Rosa-Mendoza
Illustrator: Lindy Burnett

Library of Congress Cataloging-in-Publication Data

Rosa-Mendoza, Gladys.
 I live here! / by Gladys Rosa-Mendoza ; illustrated by Lindy Burnett. — School & library ed.
    p. cm. — (My world)
 Includes index.
 ISBN 978-1-60754-950-5 (library binding) — ISBN 978-1-61533-033-1 (pbk.) — ISBN 978-1-61533-034-8
(6-pack)
 1. Geography—Juvenile literature. I. Burnett, Lindy, ill. II. Title.
 G133.R65 2010
 910—dc22
                              2009054405

Manufactured in the United States of America

For more great fiction and nonfiction, go to www.windmillbooks.com

CPSIA Compliance Information: Batch #S10W: For further information contact Windmill Books, New York, New York at 1-866-478-0556.

Contents

Hi!
My name is Mark.

Let me tell you
about where I live.

I live here.
I live in a yellow house on
Wesley Street.

I live in a town called Hunt.

I have cousins who live in a city called Dallas.

Hunt is a town in the state of Texas.

The city of Dallas
is in Texas, too.

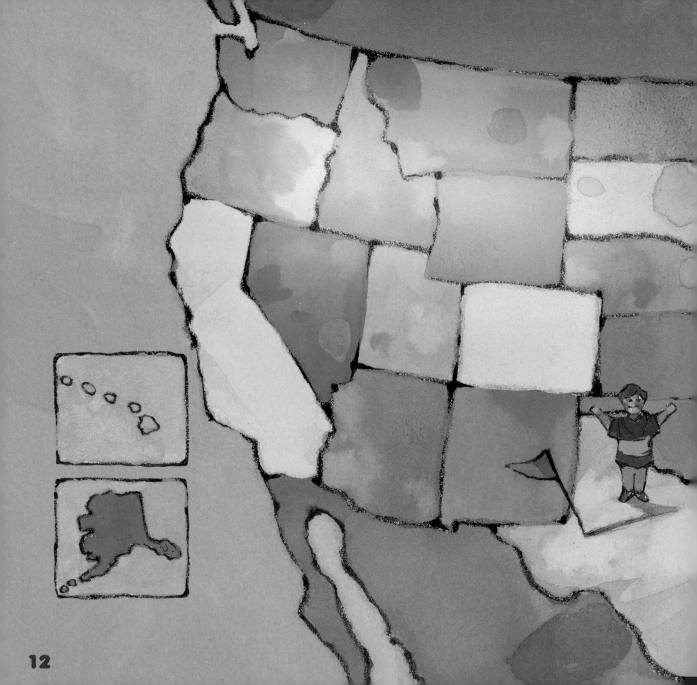

Texas is a state in
a country called
the United States
of America.

NORTH
AMERICA

EUROPE

SOUTH
AMERICA

The United
States is on
the continent
of North America.

All of the seven
continents make
up the Earth.

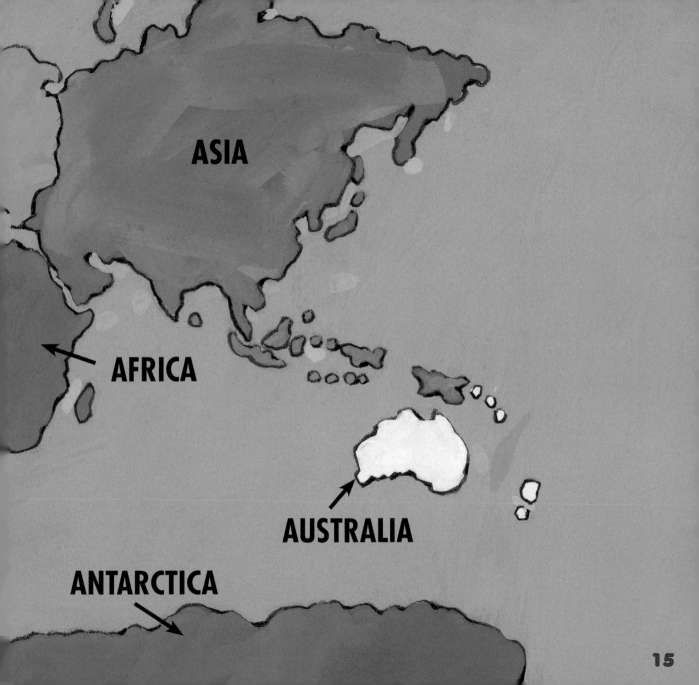

ASIA

AFRICA

AUSTRALIA

ANTARCTICA

Earth is a planet in our solar system.

Uranus

Neptune

Sun

Mercury

Venus

Earth

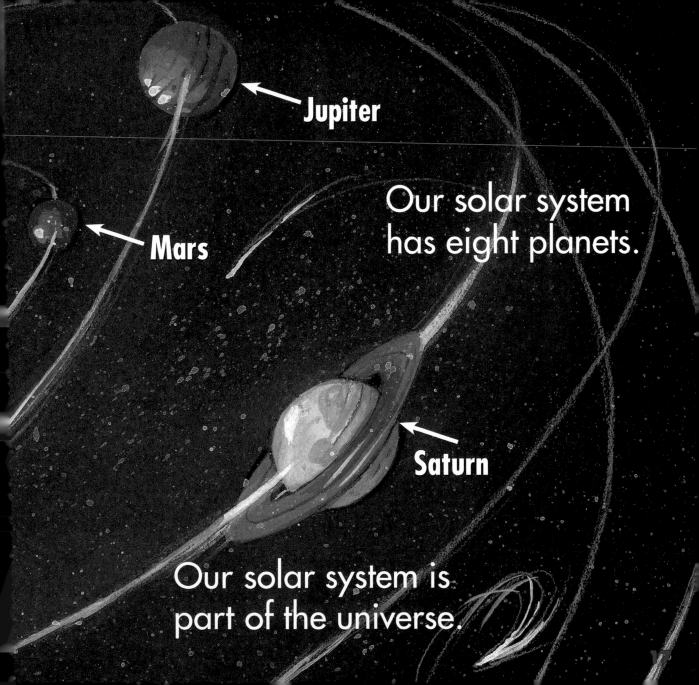

Jupiter

Mars

Saturn

Our solar system
has eight planets.

Our solar system is
part of the universe.

Washington

Oregon

Montana

North Dakota

Idaho

Wyoming

South Dakota

Nevada

Utah

Colorado

Nebraska

Kansas

Hawaii

California

Arizona

New Mexico

Oklaho

Alaska

Texas

Where do you live?

Read More!

Nonfiction

Holland, Gini. *I Live in a Town*. New York: Weekly Reader Early Learning Library, 2004.

Ljungkvist, Laura. *Follow the Line Around the World*. New York: Viking Juvenile, 2008.

Mara, Wil. *The Seven Continents*. Danbury, CT: Children's Press, 2005.

Fiction

Mayer, Mercer. *This Is My Town*. New York: HarperCollins, 2008.

Learn More!

Some cities have funny names. Did you know that there is a town in Indiana called Santa Claus?

There are more than six billion people in the world.

Do you live in a big city or a small town?

What is the farthest trip you have taken away from home?

Words to Know

city (SIH-tee) a place that is larger than a town, and usually has lots of buildings and people

continent (KON-tih-nent) one of the seven large pieces of land in the world

country (KUN-tree) an area of land that has its own government and culture

cousin (KUH-zin) the children of you aunts and uncles

house (hows) a building where a family lives

planet (PLA-nit) a large body of matter that circles around the Sun

solar system (SO-ler sis-tum) a grouping of planet and stars

town (town) an area of land that is usually smaller than a city and is made up of houses, schools, and businesses

state (stayt) one of the fifty divisions of the United States, each with their own government

universe (YU-nih-vers) the entire system of planets, stars, solar systems, and galaxies that exist

Index

C
city...9
continent...14, 15
country...12
cousins...9

E
Earth...15, 16

H
house...6

N
North America...14

P
planet...15, 16

S
solar system...
   16, 17
state...10, 12

T
Texas...10, 12
town...8, 10

U
United States of
   America...12, 14
universe...17

Web Sites

For Web resources related to the subject of this book, go to:
www.windmillbooks.com/weblinks and select this book's title

DATE DUE
